French Paintings
of Three Centuries
from the New Orleans
Museum of Art

French Paintings
of Three Centuries
from the New Orleans
Museum of Art

Organized by
the New Orleans Museum of Art
1991

Circulated by
The Trust for Museum Exhibitions,
Washington, D.C.

French Paintings
of Three Centuries
from the New Orleans
Museum of Art

Organized by the New Orleans Museum of Art 1991
Circulated by The Trust for Museum Exhibitions, Washington, D.C.

3000 copies of the catalog were published for the exhibition
French Paintings of Three Centuries from the New Orleans Museum of Art.

Exhibition Itinerary:

The Dixon Gallery and Gardens, Memphis	January 5-March 1, 1992
Center for the Fine Arts, Miami	March 15-May 3, 1992
Delaware Art Museum, Wilmington	May 17-June 29, 1992
Edsel and Eleanor Ford House, Grosse Point Shores, Michigan	July 22-September 6, 1992
Oklahoma City Art Museum	October 4-November 15, 1992
Seattle Art Museum	December 17, 1992-February 14, 1993

ISBN 0-89494-035-X

Library of Congress Catalog Card Number: 91-50764

Designed by Ed Biggs, New Orleans

Photographs by Owen Murphy, New Orleans

Printed by Balding + Mansell, Wisbech, England

Cover illustration: Charles Joseph Natoire, *The Toilet of Psyche* (cat. no. 7)

Frontispiece: François Boucher, *The Surprise* (cat. no. 5)

Contents

The New Orleans Museum of Art was founded in 1910 by Isaac Delgado, a local sugar magnate and philanthropist, for whom the Museum was named until 1971. At the time of the opening, the Isaac Delgado Museum of Art was the third art museum to be established in the southern United States. The original Delgado building was a handsome Beaux-Arts structure, "inspired by the Greek sufficiently modified to give a subtropical appearance," in the words of the architect Samuel A. Marx. In 1971, the Museum was tripled in size with the addition of three new wings. In January 1991 ground was broken for another expansion to add 50,000 square feet of new space, primarily for the display of the permanent collection. The current building program, requiring the closure of much of the present facility, has prompted the organization of this exhibition of thirty-eight French paintings from the Museum's holdings.

From the beginning, the Museum has consistently exhibited and collected French art, reflecting the strong historical and cultural ties between Louisiana and France. While numerous works have been purchased in recent years, the Museum has built its French collection principally through gifts from individual donors. In addition to paintings, the Museum also has an extensive collection of drawings and sculpture by French artists.

For the opening in 1911, the Museum borrowed a variety of works from local collectors, since no permanent collection yet existed. The most important inaugural loan was the collection of French paintings and sculptures by nineteenth–century Barbizon and Salon artists belonging to Mr. and Mrs. Chapman H. Hyams. The forty works in the Hyams collection were bequeathed to the Museum in 1915, forming the cornerstone of its French collection. Another early exhibition, presented in 1912, featured the work of the French Impressionists, organized by the Paris art dealer Durand-Ruel. This exhibition was initiated by Hunt Henderson, a New Orleans collector and later Museum Trustee, who, beginning around 1900, had formed the earliest collection of the French Impressionists in the South, including five paintings each by Monet and Renoir. While the Hunt Henderson collection now has been dispersed, the collector's son, Charles C. Henderson donated a Degas pastel and Renoir oil to the Museum in the 1970s.

After the initial excitement of the opening of the Museum, there was little growth of the permanent collection between the two World Wars. The only important work by a French artist acquired by the Museum during those years was the large *Toilet of Psyche* by Natoire. Originally brought to America in 1815 by the exiled Joseph Bonaparte, it was acquired in 1845 by the New Orleans banker James Robb, making it at the time the best known example of Rococo painting in America. It was only in 1948 with the appointment of the Museum's first full-time professional director, Alonso Lansford, that the real growth of the French collection began with the acquisition of works by twentieth–century School of Paris masters.

Among the cultural connections between Louisiana and France were the annual visits to New Orleans during the nineteenth century of many French artists, primarily portraitists seeking commissions. Although he came for personal reasons, certainly the greatest of these visiting artists was Edgar Degas, who spent the winter of 1872-73 with his maternal relatives in New Orleans. During his visit, Degas painted a dozen or more works at the home of his uncle Michel Musson, a prominent cotton merchant whose house still stands on Esplanade Avenue just fifteen blocks from the Museum. The first work by Degas to enter the Museum's collection was a bronze sculpture of a horse given by the Musson family in 1950. In 1965, during the directorship of James B. Byrnes, the Museum acquired through public subscription the large portrait of Estelle Musson, the artist's first cousin, painted during his visit. The excitement aroused by the Museum's purchase of this painting focused the City's attention on the Museum as never before, making possible its future growth and expansion. Interestingly Degas was not the only great French artist with family in New Orleans. Odilon Redon's mother also was a native of New Orleans, who married a Frenchman briefly in residence in the City. Unfortunately Redon never visited his maternal relatives in Louisiana, a place that surely would have inspired his Symbolist imagery.

The decades of the 1970s and 1980s witnessed the rapid growth of the Museum's French collection. The 1974 bequest of Victor K. Kiam added significant paintings and sculptures by School of Paris artists; while the 1986 bequest of long-time Trustee Muriel Bultman Francis greatly enriched the collection of French drawings, including eight sheets by Ingres. While collectors have been generous in donating works by nineteenth- and twentieth-century artists, the Museum has purchased most of the important paintings by seventeenth- and eighteenth-century masters. These acquisitions have significantly broadened the Museum's survey of four centuries of French art. Perhaps the most important of these purchases, acquired to celebrate the Museum's 75th anniversary, was the life-size 1788 portrait of *Marie Antoinette, Queen of France*, by Elisabeth Vigée–Lebrun, which due to its size could not be included in this exhibition.

The New Orleans Museum of Art is delighted to share this selection of its French paintings with six of its sister institutions throughout the United States. We are grateful to the Directors of these museums for agreeing to host the exhibition. Special thanks are due to Ann Van Devanter Townsend and her staff at The Trust for Museum Exhibitions in Washington, D.C., for so ably handling all of the myriad details involved in organizing and circulating this

show. I am happy to acknowledge the fine work of those individuals who contributed to this catalog: in particular, Professor Marilyn R. Brown of Tulane University, who wrote the insightful introduction; and, on our staff, Sharon E. Stearns, Curatorial Researcher, who wrote a number of the catalog entries, and revised earlier entries by the late Edward P. Caraco, Curator of European Art; and Kathleen Doll,

Foreword and Acknowledgements

Secretary to the Director, who prepared the manuscript.

This exhibition of three centuries of French Painting exemplifies the rich cultural heritage that characterizes one of America's most unique cities. It is the hope of the Trustees and staff of the New Orleans Museum of Art that the thousands of people who view this exhibition during its American tour may one day visit New Orleans to see our Museum after the opening of the expanded facility in the Spring of 1993.

E. John Bullard
Director

t is appropriate that the French paintings in this exhibition were produced during an historical period when political and, subsequently, cultural links between New Orleans and France were firmly established. As social constructions, these pictures bear witness to the rich complexity of the city's French heritage, as well as to the heterogeneous development of the visual arts in France from the seventeenth to the end of the nineteenth century.

In 1682, the explorer La Salle claimed an area of land surrounding the Mississippi River for France and named it Louisiana in honor of King Louis XIV. In 1718, Bienville founded New Orleans, naming it for the Duke of Orleans, regent of the Kingdom. France ceded New Orleans and the Louisiana Territory west of the Mississippi to Spain in 1763, following the end of the Seven Years' War, but Napoleon later forced Spain to retrocede Louisiana according to the second Treaty of San Ildefonso of 1800. When Napoleon's imperialistic plans for the Caribbean went awry, he decided to negotiate with the Americans so as to keep the British from controlling the New World. Although the Louisiana Purchase of 1803 (and Louisiana's subsequent statehood in 1812) effectively ended New Orleans' political ties with France, cultural exchanges continued to flourish during the nineteenth century (see cat. no. 7, purchased by a local collector in 1845, and cat. no. 23, painted in New Orleans in 1872.)

The corresponding early modern era of French history ranged from a period of authoritarian consolidation to one of dynamic change, visual resonances of which can be traced in paintings in this exhibition. During the seventeenth-century reigns of Louis XIII (1610-43) and the Sun King, Louis XIV (1643-1715), France was established as the most powerful national political force in Europe. Building upon the economic, cultural, and religious centralization established by Cardinals Richelieu and Mazarin, the Machiavellian first ministers of the rather weak Louis XIII, Louis XIV weathered the noble-led revolt against royal authority in 1648-53 (known as the Fronde) to establish himself as absolute monarch. The palace at Versailles (1669-88), with its axes converging on the king's chamber, became the architectural symbol of the centralized authority of the king over the aristocrats of his court. Claude Lefebvre painted his *Portrait of Louis XIV* (cat. no. 2) in 1670, when Versailles was beginning to be built. The artist represented the king as an elegant courtier whose refinement was subtended by military might, symbolized by his sword and armor, the latter studded with the royal fleur-de-lis insignia. The Sun King had defeated the Spanish in 1659, and in 1668 had successfully attacked the Spanish Netherlands. France indeed set a standard for the growing armies of Europe: at the peak of his power, Louis retained some 400,000 men under arms. It was in this imperialistic spirit that the king extended his power into Louisiana and elsewhere. Three years after La Salle's claim on the Mississippi, Louis revoked the Edict of Nantes, which, since Henri IV had issued it in 1598, had granted religious and political freedom to French Protestants, called Huguenots. Their exile subsequent to 1685 meant that the Sun King unwittingly contributed to the future cultural development of French Acadians in Louisiana, better known today as Cajuns. More immediately, his cultural centralization in France made the seventeenth century the age of Descartes, Pascal, Corneille, Racine, Molière, La Fontaine, Bossuet, and many others whose work and thought profoundly affected Western culture.

The distinctive pose Lefebvre gave to the Sun King, who is depicted standing with one hand on his hip (a table in the background holds his helmet) and the other on his staff of state, was later rotated to the left and enlarged to a full-length and more pompous stance of absolute monarchy in the well-known portrait by Hyacinthe Rigaud (1701, Paris, Louvre). Here Louis XIV was portrayed in all his dandified magnificence, his symbolic sword tucked under his heavy ermine-lined cloak, as though he were reviewing throngs of bowing courtiers ensconced at Versailles. By the time Callet painted his *Portrait of Louis XVI* (cat. no. 11) in 1782-83, the obvious echoes of Rigaud's opulent portrait of the subject's ancestor were somewhat wishful thinking. During the eighteenth-century reigns of Louis XV (1715-74) and of Louis XVI (1774-92) and his wife Marie-Antoinette (depicted by Elisabeth Vigée-Lebrun in 1788 in the New Orleans Museum's large portrait of the queen, not in the current exhibition), the royal power that had been consolidated by the Sun King was decentralized. Although this was the period known as the *ancien régime*, aristocratic courtiers retreated from Versailles, seeking their pleasure in Paris, where artists were engaged to decorate elegant salons (see cat. nos. 5 and 7 by Boucher and Natoire). Meanwhile, a prosperous middle class became so numerous that even the aristocracy began to assimilate themselves to the manners and taste of this new class (compare cat. nos. 8 and 10 by Greuze and Vincent). This was also the age of the *philosophes*, including Voltaire, Rousseau, and Diderot, whose influential Enlightenment ideas helped increase religious and political tolerance. It is, in fact, possible to see the coming of the French Revolution in 1789 both as a final flowering of an age of reform and as a cataclysm bringing just retribution to a greedy and corrupt aristocracy— a question of interpretation still avidly debated by historians.

Although the tumultuous events of the Revolutionary period itself (1789-94) are not alluded to in paintings in the current exhibition, many of its ideals found expression in the works of Jacques-Louis David. Reminiscences of the style of David linger in the work of his pupil Baron Gros, whose calligraphic brushstrokes in the *First Sketch for The Pest House at Jaffa* (cat. no. 12) recall the background of David's famous *Death of Marat* (1893,

Brussels, Musées Royaux des Beaux-Arts de Belgique). But Gros' subject matter, like that of David himself, had by 1804 shifted to embrace the political career of Napoleon (1799-1815), who in many respects personified a reversal of the democratic principles of the Revolution and a return to doctrines of imperialism. Commissioned as a Napoleonic propaganda piece to commemorate the aftermath of one of the battles that in 1799 had enabled Bonaparte to consolidate his military power and eventually overthrow the government of the Directory (1795-99), the finished painting of *Napoleon at the Pest House at Jaffa* was exhibited at the Salon of 1804.

An Introduction to French Paintings of Three Centuries

by Marilyn R. Brown

Both the New Orleans sketch, which shows the military hero holding a dying man in his arms, and the finished painting, which, reminiscent of Rembrandt's *Hundred Guilder Print*, likens Bonaparte to Christ by showing him removing a glove to touch the sore of a plague victim, evidently embroidered considerably upon historical events in order to fabricate a Napoleonic mythology. As art historian Norman Schlenoff has related, one witness account suggested that Bonaparte actually walked quickly across the room and avoided contact with the sick; another claimed that he did touch the plague victims in order to persuade his own soldiers that there was no contagion; but it seems that a Dr. Desguenettes (who stands to the right of Napoleon in the final version) had already vaccinated himself and, presumably, Bonaparte against infection.

Between the New Orleans sketch and the final painting, Gros opened up the closed room to a more exotic setting (near present-day Tel Aviv), which added to the Emperor's romantic appeal. The extremes of emotion expressed by Gros in the gestures of the sick and dying (which were to have such an impact on Gericault's politically more democratic painting *The Raft of the Medusa*, 1819, Paris, Louvre) meanwhile heralded a turning away from the rationality of the Enlightenment. The Napoleonic cult of the hero (compare Wicar's brooding portrait of one of Napoleon's officers, cat. no. 13) was, even after Waterloo, to have broader ramifications for Romanticism, when the principle of bourgeois individualism and the artistic cult of the genius came into full prominence.

After the demise of Napoleon, the remainder of the nineteenth century was a period of political turbulence. French revolutions recurred in 1830, 1848, and 1871, commemorated artistically by, among others, Delacroix, Meissonier, and Manet. The Bourbon Restoration (1815-30) was followed in succession by the July Monarchy (1830-48), the Second Republic (1848-51), the Second Empire (1851-70), the Commune (1871), and the Third Republic (beginning in 1871). As bourgeois democracy was gradually won, kings and heroes began to disappear from painting, displaced by other, more modern historical forces.

Most notable in respect to the current exhibition was the direct relationship between the growth of the Industrial Revolution and the burgeoning of French landscape painting, ranging from the romantic Naturalism of Barbizon artists like Diaz (cat. no. 16) to the materialist Realism of Courbet (cat. no. 14). Robert Herbert has discussed how, as actual rural landscapes were increasingly encroached upon by expanding cities and industrial sprawl, landscape painting gained a new social and aesthetic value as a needed outlet for a distinctly urban vision. Some landscapists like Corot (cat. no. 15) filtered nature through nostalgic memory, reviving the calm, atmospheric glow of classical seventeenth-century French landscapes, most notably the arcadian ideal of Claude (see cat. no. 1). Other artists, especially those of the Impressionist generation, sought a landscape that was more consciously modern. Boudin, like his protégé Monet, could upon occasion include signs of industry at the edges of otherwise peaceful scenes of river villages (see cat. no. 25). The late work of Pissarro, an anarchist who espoused a rural ideal of community life, offers an interesting dialectic of country and city scenes (see cat nos. 29, 30). Once Monet could afford to live outside of Paris, whose crowded boulevards and steaming railroad stations he had depicted when the Impressionists first began exhibiting there in the 1870s, he increasingly transformed his vision of nature into a private realm of individual sensation. In so doing, he transmuted the empirical data of perception into a modernized version of the eighteenth-century ideal of *sensibilité* (cat. nos. 27,28). As Monet retreated increasingly into Normandy, his colleague Sisley returned to the rural sites around Fontainebleau forest that had appealed to the earlier generation of Barbizon artists (compare cat. nos. 26 and 16).

In different ways the Post-Impressionist generation continued the retreat from the modern historical forces of urban industrialization. Gauguin chose to pursue ideals of the noble savage, derived from the Enlightenment writings of Rousseau, and notions of the exotic, inherited from the Napoleonic era. In rural Brittany (see cat. nos. 33, 34) and then Tahiti he sought a primitive paradise (representations of which he paradoxically hoped would make his fortune on the Paris art market), only to find that it had already been lost to French colonialism, another bequest of the eighteenth century. Back in Paris, while Bonnard caricatured people in the public street to the point of abstraction (cat. no. 35), Vuillard sought a private, if rather claustrophobic haven in the bourgeois interior (cat. no. 36). Here the tension between abstraction and representation, between the calm domesticity of the subject and the indeterminate nervousness of the surface texture, suggests a new psychological world in which the problematic qualities of the outer world, including instability and ambiguity, are transported to the interior. This intimist realm, with all its contradictions, was not sufficient for the Symbolist Redon, who retreated even further into the imaginary world of the dream and the unconscious (cat. nos. 37, 38) that was simultaneously being explored through more clinical, psychiatric means by his Austrian contemporary Freud.

The three centuries that take us from baroque absolutism to modernism in French painting also saw significant changes in the social and economic contract between the artist, the State, and the public. This era encompassed the rise and fall of a centralized arts administration in France. The fine arts division of the French Academy was officially founded under the auspices of Louis XIV's powerful minister Colbert in 1664, as a means of establishing State support and control. As we have seen, the seventeenth century was an authoritarian age of court patronage. An official hierarchy of artistic genres was established, with history painting placed at the top and landscape at the bottom — a ranking that was obviously reversed by the late nineteenth century.

To understand how this occurred, one can look to changes in patronage in the intervening years. With the decentralization of the aristocrats and the growth of the bourgeoisie in the eighteenth century, there was a demand for less grandiose pictures; smaller rooms required smaller paintings; more informal behavior elicited art to provide an appropriate setting. Meanwhile, as Thomas Crow has examined, the institution of annual Salons (State-sponsored art exhibitions) in 1737 created a new public discourse about art. Art criticism was born and was practiced by journalists and intellectuals ranging from Saint-Yenne to Diderot — a tradition continued in the nineteenth century by such lettered critics as Stendhal, Baudelaire, and Zola. During the eighteenth century, Diderot praised artists like Greuze (see cat. no. 9) and Chardin for painting middle-class virtues rather than what he saw as the decadence of the aristocratic Rococo (compare cat. no. 5). Leaving behind Diderot's invocation of morality, Baudelaire continued in the mid-nineteenth century to call for a "painter of modern life."

Even though the Academy was temporarily abolished under the auspices of David and the French Revolution, it was soon reinstated. The Salon continued to be a major source of patronage throughout the nineteenth century, until its dominance was effectively ended by the creation of an artist-organized Salon des Indépendents in 1884. The standards of the official Salon, conservatively based on the classical ideals and hierarchies of the seventeenth century, soon were out of step with the kind of art that was increasingly being demanded by the triumphant middle class. Alternative forms of patronage were concomitantly created in the form of commercial art dealers, ranging from Martinet to Durand-Ruel, without whose support those artists such as the Impressionists, who dissented from Academic standards, could not have survived. As Robert Herbert and Nicholas Green have argued, entrepreneurial dealers increasingly fostered a bourgeois market whose clients were willing to risk investment in innovative art in the hope of future vindication. The progressive paintings they purchased incrementally expressed the individualistic ideals of these new clients, as well as of the artists who produced them, rather than the collective standards of the Academy. Landscape, rather than history painting, increasingly responded to the feelings and aspirations of a largely urban and industrial middle-class public. Through changes in patronage, then, the style and subjects of French paintings were historically linked with larger political, social, and economic currents.

Despite the trajectory of historical changes in French painting and its social contract over three centuries, there are leitmotifs that provide for continuity in viewing the current exhibition. The so-called quarrel of the ancients and moderns that had its origins in the seventeenth century continued to reverberate in the nineteenth. In the seventeenth century the Academy embraced the solemn classicism of Poussin: painting was considered a rational expression of serious and elevating ideas, a means of intellectual communication rather than emotional expression. Subjects were chosen from ancient history, classical literature, or religion; seductive color (which was feminine: *la couleur*) was submitted to the crisp control of line (which was masculine: *le dessin*); and the spiraling spatial expansiveness of the Rubensian baroque style was restrained by a more severely Poussinist rectilinearity (see Colombel's *Adoration*, cat. no. 3, based on an earlier composition by Poussin). As in the classical literature of Corneille and Racine, the decorum of strict rules provided for an appropriate expression of an age of absolutism. But there were strains of lyricism, even within seventeenth-century classicism, most notably in the idyllic pastoral landscapes of Claude (cat. no. 1). Where Poussin sought rationality, Claude found atmospheric emotions and filtered sensations that would be revived in the *sensibilité* of the Rococo and the picturesque ideal of Romanticism.

During the eighteenth century, proponents of the Rococo style revived the baroque over the classical sensibility and could opt either for ancient or more immediately modern topics and find similarities between them (compare Natoire's *Toilet of Psyche*, cat. no. 7 and Boucher's *Surprise*, cat. no. 5). Tensions between the ancient and the modern became more pronounced again in the nineteenth century, when the Academy promoted a by now *retardataire* Neoclassicism in the face of more progressively contemporary styles and subjects (compare Bouguereau, cat. no. 22 and Degas, cat. no. 23).

A corollary of the dialectic of ancient and modern was that of finish and sketch. Artists trained in the Academic traditions of the Ecole des Beaux-Arts learned how to do preliminary sketches (see cat. no. 12) with the understanding that a final version would be completed with the meticulous, classical finish that, from Poussin onwards, connoted rational adherence to a collective discipline and work well-done (see cat. no. 3). In private, rather than official public art, painters in the eighteenth century, ranging from the Rococo to bourgeois realism, could employ a more painterly execution to various ends. In the case of Boucher (cat. no. 5), the sketchlike licks of the brush could supply a visual correlative for a more literal delectation of the erotic subject. (This erotics of the brush was continued in the nineteenth century, most famously by Renoir, cat. no. 32). In the case of Greuze (whose morals Diderot preferred to Boucher's), a fairly crisp finish, despite painterly details, could be employed for a commissioned aristocratic portrait (cat. no. 8), while a more rugged *facture* could be deemed appropriate to evoke the humble sincerity of the lower social classes (cat. no. 9).

By the early nineteenth century, the generative (or sketch) phase of painting was increasingly privileged over the executive phase (or finish) by progressive artists like Delacroix. As Albert Boime has suggested, the "abstract" qualities of the Academic sketch (the *esquisse*, *étude*, and *ébauche*) were believed by the Romantics to be more closely expressive of the originality and individuality of the artist, which, it was thought, could only be stifled by Academic rules of line and finish. It is not surprising that Delacroix once owned Gros's *First Sketch for The Pest House at Jaffa* (cat. no. 12), especially given the degree to which its rich color oppositions of greenish blues and warm reds bring Delacroix's palette to mind. The more meticulous polish (and Italianate format) of Wicar's *Portrait of Colonel Durosnel* (cat. no. 13) exemplifies, on the other hand, the Neoclassical features steadfastly conserved by artists in the circle of Ingres, Delacroix's proverbial rival.

With the emergence of Naturalist and Impressionist landscape painting in the middle and latter portions of the nineteenth century, the sketch (which artists like Monet, Renoir, and Sisley learned from their Academic instruction in the *atelier* of Gleyre) was further privileged for additional reasons. The Realist (and socialist) Courbet applied pigment with his palette knife like a workman with his trowel so as to approximate the concrete materiality of observed nature (cat. no. 14). Likewise opposing Academic doctrines of finish, painters of the Barbizon and Impressionist generations handled their paint in an increasingly sketchlike manner in order to combine the flicker of instantaneous perception (light broken into pure colors) with the filter of individual temperament as it identified with nature's changing moods (see cat. nos. 15, 16, 23, 26, 27, 28, 29, 30, 31). The surface of the textured canvas itself became the concordant plane of experience. The Symbolists' subsequent retreat from objective nature transformed the brushstroke into an increasingly abstract register of individual subjectivity (see cat. nos. 37, 38).

But Academic finish was still alive and well (see cat. nos. 18 and 22). While the Impressionists and Post-Impressionists were exhibiting their work independently and through commercial dealers, Salon artists like Gérôme and Vibert (cat. nos. 19, 20, 21), inspired by the invention and proliferation of photography, fabricated a slick illusion of "objective" documentation in exotic and incongruous mock-historical scenes. It has been suggested by Linda Nochlin that Gérôme's deceivingly realistic representations of North Africa and the Near East (see cat. nos. 19, 20) were just as imbricated with the ideology of French colonialism as exotic pictures from Delacroix's diplomatic visit to North Africa in 1832 or propagan-

distic celebrations of Napoleon's Near Eastern campaigns (see cat. no. 12).

A final leitmotif that can provide a sense of continuity across three centuries is the representation of women as a vehicle for the aesthetic construction of responses to larger historical and social forces. In the absence of women artists in this exhibition, we can instead observe some of the various ways women were represented by male artists. In the erotic display of female sexuality, Boucher's *The Surprise* in particular was to have reverberations for the future (cat. no. 5). Although some have suggested that Boucher invented the pin-up, this painting is more significant than that assessment implies. Caught in a triangular intersection of *liaisons dangereuses* (Laclos's novel by that name would not appear until 1782), Boucher's woman is suspended in a "cat's cradle" of innocence and experience. But there is no doubt which will triumph. Semi-reclining on cushions fit for an *odalisque* (or harem woman: Boucher would in 1746 do a related engraving for J.-A. Guer's *Moeurs et usages des Turcs*), the woman shares gazes with a young chambermaid who protectively covers her mistress' genital area with a hand. Yet the ardent expression of the male intruder, echoed rather humorously in that of the cat, dominates the pediment of human protagonists. The cat, placed provocatively in the woman's lap, conveniently assists her *décolletage*. With its erect tail signalling sexual alertness and receptivity, the cat in particular would, along with the lap dogs of related paintings by Fragonard, become, as Mary Sheriff has argued, a typical emblem in a symbolic system of erotic allusion pervasive in Rococo pictures, especially those produced for private salons. The viewer, usually presumed to identify with the male intruder, was entertained, not only by the sensual pleasure of sexual fantasy, but also by the intellectual pleasure of deciphering the play of symbols. Alternatively, in Natoire's larger and more classically inspired *Toilet of Psyche* (which some believe may have been influenced by a cycle on the same topic by Boucher), the surrogate male figure is excluded from representation (cat. no. 7). But the male viewer is offered the voyeuristic position of observing a forbidden sight (again note the harem analogy): Psyche is being prepared for her first night of love with Cupid in his palace. In neither painting does the gaze of the depicted woman meet that of the viewer.

Over a century later, Manet, in his scandalous painting *Olympia* (1863, Paris, Musée d'Orsay) was to turn the tables on the male viewer by having the depicted woman (now a prostitute) defiantly meet his gaze. Boucher's accoutrements of cushions, curtain, maid, and symbolic cat would still be present, but the protective hand over the genitals would now belong to Olympia herself. The gesture of drawing back the curtain to reveal the "truth" of sexual display would later be employed more radically by Picasso in *Les Demoiselles d'Avignon* (1907, New York, Museum of Modern Art). A more puerile meeting of the viewer's gaze can be found in Bouguereau's Neoclassical *Whisperings of Love* (cat. no. 22), where a chaste and distant descendant of Natoire's Psyche is accompanied by an infant Cupid and a Greek amphora which not only signifies archeological "exactitude," but also symbolizes the intact "vessel" of the young woman's virginity (Bouguereau, like Greuze, also pointedly depicted *The Broken Pitcher*, 1891, The Fine Arts Museums of San Francisco).

As the Bouguereau implies, the obverse of the leitmotif of woman as erotic spectacle was that of woman as domesticated angel, further examples of which can be found in the exhibition. A rather literal connection between women and the "distaff" side of family life can be found in pictures ranging from Greuze's aristocratic *Mme. Gougenot de Croissy* (cat. no. 8) with her *navette* (a decorative shuttle, rather more symbolic than practical in function), to Renoir's more bourgeois *Seamstress at Window* (cat. no.

32). Typical of many men in the eighteenth and nineteenth centuries and beyond, Renoir believed that a woman's place was in the home. (He once stated frankly, "I consider women writers, lawyers, and politicians [such as] George Sand, Madame [Juliette] Adam and other bores as monsters and nothing but five-legged calves.") Since the early eighteenth century, the Industrial Revolution sent lower-class men and women and middle-class men out of the home environment to work, fostering a treasured myth of the bourgeois home as a felicitous feminine realm. Following the Enlightenment ideas of Rousseau and others, eighteenth-century artists like Vincent (cat. no. 10) began to promote a recurring (and frequently stereotypical) image of the happy mother that borrowed explicitly from the iconography of the Madonna and Child (compare cat. no. 3). As Carol Duncan has argued, such pictures of *maternité* often bore little relation to the reality of family life and served to confirm mythic notions of the contentedness and stability of middle-class social structures.

According to Tamar Garb, the incremental popularity of images extolling cheerful fertility and "natural" domesticity (which reached something of a peak with Renoir) occurred at precisely the time women's (and mother's) legal power was being severely curtailed. Napoleon, in his famous exchange with the writer Madame de Staël, argued that female greatness had a single dimension — childbearing. The Napoleonic Code legitimized the absolute authority of the husband by ending financial independence for wives and by giving mothers no legal authority over children during the father's lifetime. Female adultery was punished while that of males was condoned. Women were prevented from filing paternity suits or standing as legal witnesses. The notion of maternity was restricted to the biological functions of reproduction and the child care which was thought to be a "natural" extension of the former.

In view of these historical circumstances, it would be something of a relief to turn to the intervention of women Impressionists like Morisot and Cassatt in the tradition of representing maternity. In the absence of their works in this exhibition (though not in the New Orleans Museum of Art), it is equally gratifying to turn to an important work by their male colleague Degas, who, like them, was attuned to the emergence of French feminism during the latter part of the nineteenth century, although he responded in a more paradoxical manner. In his series of genre scenes of working-class laundresses, milliners, dancers (see cat. no. 24), bathers, and prostitutes, he could respond to women as creatures of the aesthetic and, in the case of the latter, erotic display. But, as Norma Broude, Eunice Lipton, Carol Armstrong, Charles Bernheimer, and others have argued, the frequent accusation of misogyny in Degas' case is a mistake. Even while exploring dominant sexual stereotypes, he continually demythologized and often de-eroticized them; and, in his portraits of middle-class women from the circle of his family and friends, he, unlike Renoir, offered memorably sympathetic representations of female individuality. Conventional images of maternity and domesticity are rare in his work. Even though he represented his New Orleanian cousin and sister-in-law Estelle Musson DeGas when she was pregnant with her fourth child (cat. no. 23), the point of the portrait was not to celebrate happy motherhood. Although there was an iconographic tradition drawing symbolic parallels between the supposedly "natural" fecundity of women and that of flowers and fruit, Degas managed to subvert the stereotype. He masked his subject's swelling abdomen in a mournful dress and shifted the viewer's attention to the poignant, yet unsentimentalized, situation of a woman who was nearly blind (she had contracted opthalmia in 1866, had lost the vision in her left eye in 1868, and would lose that of her right eye in 1875) arranging intensely colored flowers by touch in a blurred and darkened room. Despite the presence of a window, the spatial compression and hint of claustrophobia in the scene look forward to Vuillard (cat. no. 36). Degas himself had by this point in his life contracted eye problems that would leave him with essentially monocular vision. He represented his cousin primarily as a fellow-suffering human being who also happened to be a woman. The humanity of this and the other paintings in this exhibition still resonates today.

NOTES TO THE CATALOG:

The paintings are arranged in a generally chronological order. Dimensions are given in centimeters and inches, height preceding width. The authors of individual entries are indicated by their initials: S.E.S. — Sharon E. Stearns; E.P.C. — Edward P. Caraco; J.G.C. — Joan G. Caldwell. An index of artists and titles appears at the end of the catalog.

1 Claude Gelée, called Claude Lorrain (1600-1682)

Little is known of the formative years of Claude, who would become one of the most reknowned landscape painters in the history of European art. His birth-place is likely Chamagne, in the duchy of Lorraine and he is known to have gone to Rome while still an adolescent as an apprentice to a pastry maker. His earliest artistic encounter was with the painter Agostino Tassi, in whose household he was employed. Recent biographers have pointed out the influence on his work of the luministic effects visible in landscape painting from the German-born Goffredo Wals and the Fleming Paul Brill. Claude's first Roman works from the early 1630s were fresco cycles, but by the end of the decade he was the principal landscape painter in Italy, having received commissions from the highest ranking ecclesiastics and the King of Spain.

The subject here is pastoral: shepherds and their herd return home at the end of the day. Behind them rises the first-century B.C. Temple of the Sibyl at Tivoli, rendered accurately in its ruinous state. Claude has changed the general topography of this location in the Roman campagna to accomodate his classic landscape construction: foreground area, subtle gradations of spatial recession with trees used as repoussoirs, a major land mass in the middle of the composition and an extended vista to one side. The temple, cascade and medieval fortifications help set the scene of an idyllic past, while the small representation of St. Peter's on the horizon links the image to the actuality of contemporary urban Rome. The emotional quality of the landscape is brought forth by the atmospheric effects of the light and the colorful sky, brilliantly rendered in the golden sunset and in its reflections on the clouds.

The *Ideal View of Tivoli* corresponds with drawing 81 in Claude's *Liber Veritatis* (London, British Museum), a collection of drawings started by Claude about 1637 to record his more important painted compositions. This drawing is dated 1644 and is inscribed on the verso *taublaux pour paris*, most likely indicating a Parisian patron. A similar composition with the same setting at Tivoli has been used by Claude in 1642 for the *Landscape with Tobias and the Angel* (private collection; *Liber Veritatis* drawing no. 65). A third version entitled *Landscape with Shepherds* (Fine Arts Museums of San Francisco), whose attribution is now questioned, has varying elements in the landscape, though there is no known drawing connected with it.

E.P.C.

Ideal View of Tivoli, 1644
oil on canvas
117 x 147 cm. / 46 x 57 ⅞ inches
Museum Purchase,
78.1

2   Claude Lefebvre (1632-1675)

Few paintings remain from the prodigious output of Lefebvre. He studied painting with his father at Fontainebleau, was later a student of Claude de Höey and spent a year in the studio of Eustache Le Sueur before entering Charles Le Brun's studio in 1655 where he was encouraged to pursue portraiture. Lefebvre's reception piece upon admission to the Royal Academy in 1663 was the robust portrait of Colbert now at Versailles. During the early years of the Sun King's reign, Lefebvre was second only to Philippe de Champaigne in popularity as a court portraitist.

This late portrait by Lefebvre reveals how he abandoned the stark simplicity and polished realism of Champaigne's style for a freer, more painterly style closer to that of Le Brun. Louis' armor, studded with golden fleurs de Lys, and great silver-blue sash sparkle with reflected light. Lefebvre also takes pleasure in rendering the textures of fur, feathers and the King's great wig. The three-quarter length format and the stylized posture are taken from earlier Flemish portraits in the Baroque style.

The Sun King is represented here at age thirty-two, when his first plans for the palace of Versailles were being realized. Despite the military garb and the accoutrements of power, the King's love of elegance and refinement appear essential to his personality. Lefebvre seems to have captured the vital trait that made Louis the most powerful ruler in his day - an understanding of his own destiny as concomitant with his grand designs for the realm.

E.P.C.

Portrait of Louis XIV, King of France, 1670
oil on canvas
116.8 x 89.5 cm. / 46 x 35¼ inches
Gift of the Hirschl
and Adler Gallery, New York,
56.67

3   Nicolas Colombel (1644-1717)

Colombel was born near Rouen in 1644 and was in Rome by 1682 when he sent four large paintings to Paris. In 1686 he was made a member of the Roman Academy of St. Luke; sometime between then and 1693 he made his way back to Paris. In 1694 he was *reçu* at the Royal Academy and exhibited many works at the Salons of 1699 and 1704. Colombel's oeuvre includes mythological, Roman and biblical paintings executed in a classicizing style strongly influenced by the work of Nicolas Poussin.

Colombel has placed the Magi and their retinue in a relief-like arrangement, in a composition taken in reverse from Poussin's *Adoration* of 1633 (Dresden, Staatliche Kunstsammlungen), though he enlarged the size of the figures and limited their number. Realism and vivid colors are balanced with an emphasis on linear design, which many of Colombel's contemporaries had abandoned. Colombel evokes an animated feeling of wonder and adoration in which all movement is directed toward the Christ child; this movement is enhanced by a clear, bright light that falls on the Madonna and child.

The painting may have been executed as long as ten years before it was first exhibited at the Salon of 1704. This practice of delayed exhibition was not unusual for Colombel who preferred to show his works in groups rather than individually at each Salon.

E.P.C.

Adoration of the Magi 1693-1699

oil on canvas

114.3 x 148.6 cm./ 45 x 58 ½ inches

Museum Purchase: Women's Volunteer Committee Fund,

73.209

4   Nicolas de Largillière (1656-1746)

Largillière was born in Paris, the son of a hat merchant; the family moved to Antwerp when he was three years old. He served as an apprentice under the Flemish painter Antoni Goubau and became a master in the Antwerp Guild of St. Luke in 1673. Two years later he was in London, in contact with several Flemish artists and Sir Peter Lely, though he was not a member of the latter's workshop as is commonly believed. Only still-lifes are documented from this early period; by the time Largillière returned to France in 1679 he had begun painting portraits, the genre for which he became celebrated. Largillière became the favorite portraitist of the Parisian *haute bourgeoisie* and executed several important commissions for Parisian municipal officials before his reception at the Royal Academy in 1699.

Largillière portrays himself here in an animated pose, pointing to a canvas in progress that depicts an Annunciation: its inclusion may refer to the academic hierarchy, which ranked history painting above portraiture. The loose treatment of the velvet coat, white shirt and wig and the accentuated foreshortening of the hand bespeak the artist's Flemish training. This realism is balanced with the tradition of formal artifice that marks the art of Hyacinthe Rigaud, the official court portraitist of the day. The painting thus exemplifies the characteristics of Largillière's style that secured success with his clients and denotes his importance in the history of French portraiture. As Myra Nan Rosenfeld has pointed out, this synthesis of the idealization of court portraiture and the realism of middle-class portraiture produced unique paintings with lasting visual appeal that herald the transition to the Rococo style.

E.P.C.

Self-Portrait, 1711
oil on canvas
81.3 x 66 cm./32 x 26 inches
Museum Purchase: Women's
Volunteer Committee Fund
in memory of Frederick M. Stafford,
82.164

5   François Boucher (1703-1770)

A fashionable painter embodying the frivolity and elegant superficiality of the French aristocratic life that engendered the Rococo, Boucher was the leading French artist of the middle of the eighteenth century. His expansive skill enabled him to master not only all of the popular painting genres of his day — mythological and religious scenes, landscapes, pastorals, portraits, and scenes from everyday life — but also design for fans and slippers as well as stage settings for the theater and ballet. So illustrious was his repute that his influence affected interior decoration, tapestry design, graphic arts, and porcelains. Boucher's talent was acknowledged by the award to him in 1724 of the coveted *prix de Rome*, in 1765 the title of First Painter of the King, and a professorship at the Royal Academy. A further honor was his standing as teacher and favorite artist of Mme. de Pompadour, the favorite of King Louis XV and the great arbiter of artistic taste in France at that time.

In its *galant* nature, depicting an idealized, but entirely possible staging of the psychological and emotional conditions of love, *The Surprise* parallels the amorous preoccupations of the Rococo age. Tension here intrudes upon the usual blissful world of Boucher in the presence of the voyeur occupying the shadows behind the young woman who reclines *en déshabillé*. Examination of the expected features, the delight in contrasting surface patterns and textures and the broken, flickering touch of the brush, identify *The Surprise* as one of the earliest works in Boucher's oeuvre, conferring upon it an important position in the establishment of the development of his painting style.

S.E.S.

The Surprise (Woman with a Cat), 1730-32
oil on canvas
81.5 x 65.5 cm./ 32 x 25 ¾ inches
Museum Purchase: Women's
Volunteer Committee Fund,
84.58

6   Charles-André Van Loo, called Carle Vanloo (1705-1765)

Of the large number of painters in the Vanloo family, Netherlandish in origin, Carle must be viewed as the most successful and highly considered of them all in the eighteenth century. As an adolescent he accompanied his brother Jean-Baptiste from Nice to Rome and studied with the painter Luti and the sculptor Le Gros. He enrolled at the Royal Academy in Paris in 1719 and was awarded the *prix de Rome* in 1724, though his seven-year stay in the Eternal City did not begin until 1727. His reputation was already considerable when he returned to Paris and he was admitted to the Academy in 1735, the year of this painting. He eventually filled every position at the Academy, was ennobled in 1751, directed the *Ecole Royale des Elèves Protégés* and, in 1762, attained the greatest artistic achievement in the realm - selection as First Painter of the King.

Vanloo's subjects were universal in scope; he worked in all genres except the less considered ones of landscape and still-life. He was most celebrated for his history paintings in which he followed the grand manner of graceful design and elevated sentiments. Such is the case with the *Noli Me Tangere*; the clarity and brightness of the colors and the sureness and precision of his drawing relate Vanloo's style to the Carracci, Guido Reni, Nicolas Poussin and Charles Le Brun. Vanloo's is an art that can be interpreted as a culminating point in the development of the classicizing style initiated in the High Renaissance.

The subject is taken from the Gospel of John and the iconography is traditional. The scene represents one of the three appearances of Christ between the Resurrection and the Ascension. The Magdalene had gone to mourn in solitude at Christ's tomb. There she noticed a gardener who spoke to her and revealed himself as Christ. She reached out to touch him, but He stopped her saying, "Touch me not, for I am not yet ascended to my Father" (John:20:17).

E.P.C.

Noli Me Tangere, 1735
oil on canvas
64.8 x 48.8 cm./ 25 ½ x 19 ¼ inches
Museum Purchase,
83.2

7   Charles Joseph Natoire (1700-1777)

Born in Provence, Natoire worked with his father, a sculptor, before going to Paris to enter the studio of François Le Moyne. He received the *prix de Rome* in 1721; from 1723 to 1729 he was active in Rome where he enjoyed an excellent reputation. Upon his return to Paris he was highly patronized. In 1737 he became a professor at the Royal Academy. By mid-century he was considered one of the great artists, along with Carle Vanloo, Jean Restout and Boucher, who dominated painting in the earlier part of Louis XV's reign.

The story of Psyche, the personification of the soul, is based on *The Golden Ass* of Apuleius, recounted again in 1669 by Lafontaine in *Les Amours de Psyché et de Cupidon*. In this painting, Psyche, whose attribute of the butterfly hovers above her head, has been transported to a new palace where her handmaidens prepare her for the first meeting with her lover Cupid. Like his contemporaries, Natoire delighted in the rendering of the female nude with its accompanying coloristic possibilities. Natoire uses an animated line in his design and the whole is bathed in a warm, shimmering light. The sense of elegance and refined beauty in this work, similar to that of Boucher, is a revealing indication of the artistic aspiration and the taste of the French Rococo.

As Colin Bailey has recently documented, *The Toilet* was one of a series of four paintings on the tale of Psyche painted for the Château de la Chevrette at Saint-Denis, which predates by two years Natoire's more famous Psyche cycle in the Hôtel de Soubise in Paris.

This work has been in America since 1815, when Joseph Bonaparte arrived in Philadelphia with an extensive collection of important paintings. Sold at auction in 1845 to James Robb, a prominent New Orleans banker and art collector, the painting has been in the city since that date. A subsequent owner, Randolph Newman, lent the work to the Museum when it opened in 1911. The painting was eventually purchased for the collection in 1940.

E.P.C.

The Toilet of Psyche, 1735-36
oil on canvas
198 x 169 cm./78 x 66 ½ inches
Museum Purchase: Bequest of
Judge Charles F. Claiborne,
40.2

8   Jean-Baptiste Greuze (1725-1805)

To eighteenth-century France the art of Jean-Baptiste Greuze appeared original, unique and morally superior to the gallant and pastoral themes painted in the Rococo style. His popularity was solidly established for the rest of the century soon after he arrived in Paris from Lyon in 1750 from his training under the painter Grandon. In 1755 he caused quite a sensation at the Salon with the exhibition of his *Family Bible Reading* (Paris, Baron Rudolph Hottinger coll.). His success was so great that some contested his authorship charging that an artist so young as he could not be the painter. Throughout much of his career he was the preferred portraitist of the upper classes, but his greater historic importance lies in the didactic genre scenes he painted. These images elicited acclaim from such notable figures as Diderot who praised Greuze's work as representing the highest ideal of painting in his day.

On a trip to Italy in 1755 Greuze was in close association with Natoire at the French Academy and met Louis Gougenot, the abbé de Chezal-Benoit, who would become one of his most important patrons. Two years later Greuze returned to France and painted portraits of Gougenot's brother Georges Gougenot de Croissy (Brussels, Musées Royaux des Beaux-Arts), future *Conseiller-secrétaire* to Louis XV, and the latter's twenty year-old wife, Marie-Angelique (née de Varennes), shown here.

This early portrait displays the straightforward interpretation Greuze gave his sitters. Mme. Gougenot de Croissy's personality is conveyed by her direct gaze, charming smile and subtle tilt of the head. Greuze's superb painterly technique is evident in the various textures rendered in her costume, especially that of the lace for which he was famous. The stylish young woman holds a *navette* or decorative shuttle around which she winds her knotted string. This activity was done in public by fashionable ladies and had no function other than to emblematically represent female diligence.

E.P.C./S.E.S.

*Portrait of Marie-Angelique
Gougenot de Croissy*, 1757
oil on canvas
80 x 62.8 cm. / 31 ½ x 24 ¾ inches
Museum Purchase:
Ella West Freeman Foundation
Matching Fund, Women's
Volunteer Committee Fund
and an Anonymous Gift,
76.268

9 Jean-Baptiste Greuze (1725-1805)

Much of the praise given to Greuze's paintings evolved out of the phenomenon of *sensibilité* that during the period from 1750 to 1780 achieved the status of a cult. *Sensibilité* may be understood as a reaction against an increasingly material conception of the universe and was manifest in a heightened consciousness of things moral and emotional.

The choice of the subject of *Head of an Old Man* is indicative of this *sensibilité* tendency. Rather than painting an aristocratic figure, Greuze chose to paint an elderly person, most likely from a humble country background. The coloring, olive greys, is dark but not drab and expresses a somber emotional mood. However the paint is applied in a free and rapid manner granting the figure a fresh vitality. The lighting is not strong, but falls gently upon the old man's features to reveal the projection of his cheekbones from the shadowy depths of his gaunt neck and jaw. His gentle eyes gaze out from the play of light and shadow upon his face and seem to reveal an infinite wisdom gleaned from years of experience. Rather than being condemned for the quality of sweet sentimentality that sometimes invades his later pictures of young women, Greuze should be judged upon such unaffected and expressive works as this.

S.E.S.

Head of an Old Man, circa 1770-75
oil on paper mounted on canvas
43.2 x 33.6 cm./ 17 x 13 ¼ inches
Gift in memory of Herbert J. Harvey, Jr.
and Marion W. Harvey,
83.51

10 François André Vincent (1746-1816)

Vincent was trained by his father, a portrait miniaturist, before entering the Academy under the tutelage of Joseph-Marie Vien. Awarded the *prix de Rome* in 1758 for history painting, he went to Rome and studied under Charles Joseph Natoire from 1771 to 1775. Upon his return to Paris, he found quick success with the many portraits and classically inspired history paintings that he submitted to the annual Salons. *Agréé* at the Academy in 1777 and *reçu* in 1782, the year of this portrait, Vincent was a prodigious painter and gifted draughtsman; admiration from the court and public grew steadily. The classical and religious subjects that Vincent depicted in the 1770s and the 1780s gave way to didactic allegories after the Revolution. Portraiture, however, remained a constant interest throughout his career. His contemporaries considered him a rival to Jacques-Louis David. Historically, his oeuvre indeed serves as a revealing indication of the change in French painting that occurred between the end of the *ancien régime* and the beginning of the Napoleonic era.

The sitter of this portrait has not been identified, but her clothing and bearing bespeak the assurance of an aristocrat. She is portrayed in an intimate moment with her child, dressed in a costume strictly reserved for home wear. Vincent presents the sitter in a straightforward and naturalistic manner, his attention given to the clarity of design and power of illusion. While the painting's surface is rich and lively, considerable care is evident in the rendering of the details of coiffure and clothing which relates the painting to earlier Rococo portraits, such as those by Greuze.

The fashion of the mother and child portrait, called a *maternité*, had become popular in France during the two decades preceeding the Revolution. In this painting Vincent has captured a sense of maternal kindness and duty in the woman's demeanor that correspond to contemporary moral attitudes about the family. This sentiment is often found in the writings of Rousseau and is clearly described by Diderot in his article on mothers in the *Encyclopédie*, volume IX.

E.P.C.

Portrait of a Mother and Child, 1782
oil on canvas
82.5 x 76.9 cm. / 32 ½ x 27 ¾ inches
Museum Purchase: Women's
Volunteer Committee Fund,
83.2

11 Antoine François Callet (1741-1823)

Callet was, as was his contemporary J.-M. Vien, the teacher of J.-L. David, one of the artists particularly active in the revival of the antique which occurred at the end of the eighteenth century and was perfected in David's severe Neo-Classical paintings. It was Callet's scenes of antique mythology and history painting that earned him his initial recognition, the *prix de Rome,* in 1764 and admission to the Royal Academy in 1780. However, his best work is in the realm of portraiture, the masterpieces of which are those he painted of King Louis XVI. His portraits are made expressive by his precise designs and brilliant coloring. Callet's early efforts at reviving the grandeur of the art of the Greeks and Romans make him an apostle of the tendencies that came to the forefront of artistic concern at the beginning of the nineteenth century.

This three-quarter length portrait, related to a full-length version housed in Versailles, depicts Louis XVI several years prior to the French Revolution. As such Louis is portrayed still secure in his power, in the pose and with the accouterments traditionally associated with royal portraits. He stands wearing full coronation regalia adorned with the fleur-de-lis, the distinctive bearing of the royal house of France. His robes part to reveal the sword of state sheathed at his hip and in the chair beside him lie the crown and double sceptor. Callet has painted this image in a manner befitting the grandeur of that which it depicts. He has spared no effort in conveying the opulence of the textures and surfaces, the intricate patterns of the laces, the gleaming gilts and satins, the soft velvets and the lustrous ermine. The elaborately carved, original frame bears an inscription revealing the portrait to have been a gift from the King to the Baron de Viomenil in 1783. This indicated the King's approval of Callet's portrait of which several were probably commissioned for use as royal gifts.

S.E.S.

Portrait of Louis XVI, King of France,
circa 1782-83
oil on canvas
162.6 x 130.8 cm./64 x 51 ½ inches
Museum Purchase: Women's
Volunteer Committee Fund
in honor of the 75th Anniversary,
86.90

12   Antoine-Jean Baron Gros (1771-1835)

Gros spent most of his youth in artistic training under his father, a portrait miniaturist. At age fifteen, he entered the studio of J.-L. David where he met J.-B. J. Wicar. By the time the Royal Academy was dissolved in 1793, Gros had never won the *prix de Rome*; ambitious and determined, he made the Italian trip on his own means. In Genoa he met Josephine Bonaparte whose influence with her brother assisted Gros in becoming a major artist to establish in paint the image of Napoleon as a military hero. Gros is one of the first French artists to be classified as a romantic because of the powerful emotional content of his works.

This oil sketch, based on a drawing in the Louvre, is a preliminary study for the monumental painting, *Napoleon at the Pest House at Jaffa* (Paris, Louvre), that was an astounding success at the Salon in 1804. The sketch portrays the actual event in March 1799 of Napoleon's visit to the hospital in Jaffa (near present-day Tel Aviv) where his troops stricken with the plague were housed. Contemporary accounts describe how the Emperor actually held a dying man in his arms. Gros' turbulent brushstroke in this study becomes an effective vehicle to portray the emotional atmosphere of the scene of suffering and despair. Yet in the midst of the dying, Napoleon appears quietly stoic.

The painting was originally commissioned as a propaganda piece; the Emperor had faced much criticism for the massacre of civilians in the Syrian campaign and it was rumored that he poisoned his own soldiers dying from the plague to avoid further contamination of his troops. This preliminary version was rejected because Napoleon felt his image was lacking in heroic qualities. The final version depicts the Emperor almost as a Christ figure, bravely touching the sores of a plague victim.

E.P.C.

First Sketch for The Pest House at Jaffa, 1804
oil on canvas
72.4 x 92.1 cm./ 28 ½ x 36 ¼ inches
Museum Purchase: Ella West Freeman Foundation Matching Fund,
67.24

13 Jean-Baptiste Joseph Wicar (1762-1834)

Wicar was a native of Lille where he began his study of painting at age ten with the artist Gueret at the Arts Academy of Lille. In 1779 city officials provided a stipend for Wicar to go to Paris to study engraving. By 1781 he had become a student of J.-L. David whom he accompanied to Rome in 1784; this same year he first exhibited his work at the Salon. He returned to France in 1793 and, through the influence of David, was named Curator of the Louvre by the revolutionary Convention. In Italy again in 1795, Wicar was appointed one of the commissioners to select works of art to be sent to Paris. At the turn of the century he settled in Rome where he painted many history paintings and portraits; he left for Naples in 1806 where he directed the Academy for three years. Wicar produced hundreds of drawings and is remembered in David's memoirs of 1825 as "the greatest draughtsman of France."

Wicar painted Durosnel in Italy sometime before August 1805 when the colonel was sent to Germany with the Grande Armée. His uniform with its silver epaulettes and buttons, dark green jacket with blue collar, cuffs and lapel piping is that of the colonel of the 16th *Chasseurs á Cheval*. Durosnel was named to this position by imperial decree on August 2, 1804, two weeks after his appointment as *Ecuyer Cavalcadour* of the Emperor. His subsequent military career was very distinguished; he eventually reached the rank of General of the Cavalry. Durosnel was made a Peer of France in 1837, served as Louis-Philippe's Aid-de-Camp and was made a member of the Legion of Honor.

The strong outlines, direct light and disciplined realism of Wicar's neoclassic style recall the art of his teacher, David. The sitter has been represented outside, with the horizon of the Italian countryside placed low in the picture field. The slightly greater than half-length format is typical of this new style of French portraiture and would be greatly exploited by Wicar's contemporaries of the early nineteenth century, particularly Ingres.

E.P.C.

Portrait of Colonel Antoine-Jean-Auguste-Henri Durosnel, 1805
oil on canvas
73.7 x 61 cm. / 29 x 24 inches
Museum Purchase: Women's
Volunteer Commiteee Fund,
83.72

14 Gustave Courbet (1819-1877)

Courbet was the son of a prosperous farming family hailing from Ornans, a small village in the east of France. In 1839 he embarked for Paris with the goal of becoming an artist. Rather than following the traditional academic course of training however, Courbet, guided by his independent character and obstinate self-assurance, followed his own course of study by copying Dutch and Spanish Old Master paintings. Although his early works reflect the Romantic tradition, by 1850, with the exhibition of his paintings *The Stone Breakers* and *The Burial at Ornans*, Gustave Courbet could legitimately be proclaimed the leader of the Realist school of painting.

Courbet is acclaimed as an innovator on account of both his subject matter and his treatment thereof. His Realist beliefs led him to choose themes from contemporary life, not excluding what was usually considered ugly or vulgar. Further, he came to eschew idealization and Romantic exoticism, preferring instead to treat his themes in an unemotional, straightforward fashion. He rejected the paint brush for the palette knife and thus rather than drawing his composition, he built it up in solid layers of paint on the canvas. Courbet acknowledged the palpable reality of the pigment, exploit-ing its materiality to construct his chosen forms and thereby convey the material reality of his subject.

Painted in Dinant, Belgium, *Rocky Landscape* exhibits Courbet's characteristic dark palette, an element he retained from his study of Old Master paintings. The surface texture betrays his confident wielding of the palette knife, the strokes particularly evident in the lower right corner. Such use of the impasto, emphasizing its materiality, is most appropriate for a landscape dominated by rock formations. The evidently palpable nature of the paint evokes the dense, solid reality of the rock. It seems appropriate then that rock, having an irrefutably material reality, plays a prominent role in Courbet's landscapes.

It is perhaps ironic that Courbet, the independent and rebellious artist who protested not only against academic teaching but as well against *any* organization of the art world, inspired a distinct school of artistic activity. Yet the guiding principle of this school, Realism, is certainly best expressed by the words of Courbet himself: "In my opinion, painting is essentially a concrete art and can only consist of reproducing real and existing things."

S.E.S.

Rocky Landscape, circa 1858

oil on canvas

52.5 x 62.5 cm./ 21 x 25 inches

Museum Purchase: Ella West Freeman Foundation Matching Fund,

69.16

15 Jean-Baptiste Camille Corot (1796-1875)

Discouraged by his family from pursuing an artistic career, Corot did not begin painting until he was twenty-six. His first training was under traditional landscape painters, but in 1825 when in Italy he began working on *plein-air* sketches. By 1827 he was showing at the annual Salons and soon thereafter joined other artists at the village of Barbizon near the Forest of Fontainebleau. Corot's name is invariably linked with the Barbizon School of landscapists who informed their canvases with a modern, fresh naturalism and a lyrical expression of their own love of the countryside; however, he actually spent relatively little time at the site. By the 1840s Corot's reputation had grown to such a point that the government acquired one of his history paintings. Financial success came in the 1850s and his popularity continued to grow, especially with the more affluent bourgeoisie.

The *Woodland Scene* displays all the characteristics of Corot's late style: matte surface, a cool palette of greys and greens and a soft atmospheric haze punctuated with spots of white and vibrant color. He creates a lyrical and nostalgic mood using a traditional landscape theme as a vehicle for personal expression. This painting may have been executed in 1872, as it bears many similarities to works such as *Landscape near Arras* (Rouen, Musée des Beaux-Arts) of that date. In that year Corot travelled throughout France and southern Belgium, painting landscapes at nearly every stop on his itinerary.

E.P.C.

Woodland Scene, 1872-1873
oil on canvas
36.8 x 59.7 cm./ 14 ½ x 23 ½ inches
Gift of Mr. and Mrs. Chapman Hyams,
15.8

16   Narcisse Virgile Diaz de la Peña (1808-1875)

Diaz de la Peña was born in Bordeaux, the son of Spanish political refugees. His family moved to Sèvres where his first artistic endeavor was, like that of Renoir, painting porcelain. After brief formal training, Diaz was first accepted in the Salon of 1835 with a history painting entitled *Battle of Medina*, derisively called at the time the Battle of the Broken Paint Pots. Two years later he was at Barbizon where he avidly took up the new style of naturalism in landscape painting. His financial success was insured by the many small works readily accepted by the Salon and quickly purchased by his bourgeois clientele. At the time of his death, Diaz had received every award that the Salon could bestow.

Diaz's oeuvre can be divided into two categories: small figural compositions of a fanciful nature that form part of the 19th-century rococo revival, and landscape views of the forest of Fontainebleau. *Autumn* belongs to the second group and is typical of his works from the late 1860s and the 1870s. It is a pure landscape, executed in earth tones, with no intruding elements from the civilized world. The sunlight creates bold patches in the clearing of the dense wood and on the treetops; the shadows are then enlivened with yellow highlights. The resulting effect is one of an enchanted landscape that embodies a sense of mystery and the quiet solitude of a purely natural setting.

E.P.C.

Autumn, 1872
oil on panel
88.9 x 76.9 cm. / 23 ¾ x 18 ¾ inches
Gift of Mr. and Mrs.
Chapman H. Hyams,
15.10

17   Félix-François-Georges-Philibert Ziem (1821-1911)

One of the most prolific artists of the nineteenth century, Ziem was originally trained as an architect in Dijon. He began painting in the mid-1840s in Paris and first exhibited at the Salon in 1848. He became a specialist in marine painting, with the waters of Venice being his favorite subject. During his early career he was under the sway of the Barbizon painters, especially Corot, but later he developed a more vibrant style with a thicker, sparkling impasto. His luminous skies and shimmering water surfaces became his trademark to his Parisian public eager to buy his work. Ziem received numerous public honors, including the rank of commander in the Legion of Honor, and was respected for his numerous philanthropic deeds.

The *Grand Canal, Venice* probably dates to the late 1860s when Ziem's brushstroke became rapid and flame-like. The material substance of the palaces along the canal appears to transform into light and color, an effect that relates Ziem's art to his contemporaries, the Impressionists. His palette is extremely vivid, causing the sky to turn into an intense blue at the top of the panel. In the distance one can see the Doge's Palace and, to the far left, the church of Santa Maria della Salute. This was Ziem's favorite view in Venice where he worked for several months every year from 1845 to 1892.

E.P.C.

Grand Canal, Venice, circa 1865-1870

oil on panel

58.4 x 85.7 cm./ 23 x 33 ¾ inches

Gift of Mr. and Mrs. Chapman H. Hyams,

15.30

18 Franz Xaver Winterhalter (1806-1873)

Although initially trained as an engraver, Winterhalter's artistic reputation rests upon his position as a prominent portrait painter of the European courts. He was born in Germany and studied engraving in both Fribourg and Munich before traveling to Paris in 1834. In Paris, under the patronage of Queen Marie-Amélie, Winterhalter quickly established his reputation through the great success with which he painted his royal sitters. Winterhalter's version of the tradition of the grand manner as inherited from Rubens and Van Dyck appealed to many more than Queen Marie-Amélie. The long list of Winterhalter's illustrious and royal sitters includes King Louis-Philippe of France and the principal members of the Orléans family, King Léopold I of Belgium, Queen Victoria of Great Britain and Prince Albert and their family, and Emperor Franz-Joseph of Austria-Hungary. This favor was due in part no doubt to his ability to capture a faithful likeness of his subjects while at the same time subtly enhancing their appearance. His most important royal patron was the Empress Eugénie into whose personal service he was pressed when Louis Napoleon Bonaparte became Emperor in 1851. Winterhalter received much reknown and many awards for the paintings he exhibited at the Salons and in 1839 was named Chevalier of the Legion of Honor.

Painted in Paris in 1850, *Young Woman in a Ball Gown* is a beautiful example of Winterhalter's depictions of the elegant figures who populated European courts. The subject enables him to indulge his skill in rendering a variety of sumptuous textures. His fluid brushwork conveys both the soft, milky flesh and the irridescent, silk taffeta ball gown with equivalent ease. Winterhalter's fancifully extravagent style appropriately documents the splendor of the imperial pretensions of Napoleon's court.

S.E.S.

Young Woman in a Ball Gown, 1850
oil on canvas
127.8 x 90 cm./51 ¼ x 38 inches
Museum Purchase: Carrie Heiderich
Fund and Gift by exchange of
Mr. and Mrs. Harris Masterson,
87.32

19   Jean-Léon Gérôme (1824-1904)

Specializing in the realm of realistic history painting, Jean-Léon Gérôme was one of the most popular artists of the nineteenth century. Until recently, however, he has been neglected and often denigrated for his realistic depictions of the oriental world of the Near East.

His paintings parallel French interest in the Arab World that began early in the nineteenth century with the publication of the nine-volume *Description d'Egypte* (1809-1829) following Napoleon's campaign and continuing with Eugene Delacroix's North African studies. Because of this popular interest, Gérôme made numerous trips to Egypt where he depicted scenes both alien and exotic to Western European eyes. This fascination with the exotic is noteworthy as one of the offshoots of the Romantic movement.

A number of paintings reveal Gérôme's distinct preference for groups of colorful figures in realistic settings. Turkish mercenaries, known as *Bashi Bazouk*, appear in paintings as merrymakers, shot casters, or, as in this painting, chess players. While another version of the *Chess Players* exists in the Wallace Collection, London, a black and red chalk drawing of the same figures can be found in the Clark Art Institute, Williamstown, Massachusetts. Of the three versions, the Museum's *Chess Players* is the most complex.

J.G.C.

Chess Players, circa 1867
oil on canvas
64.1 x 53.9 cm./ 25 ¼ x 21 ¼ inches
Gift of Mr. and Mrs.
Chapman H. Hyams,
15.14

20　Jean-Léon Gérôme (1824-1904)

Gérôme received a classical education in his native town of Vesoul before entering the Parisian studio of the history painter Delaroche. After a trip to Italy he continued his training under the Swiss-born artist Charles Gleyre, a painter of Greek and Roman subjects. It was also Gleyre who introduced Gérôme to the exotica of the Near East that fascinated the French through the nineteenth century. Gérôme's reputation was made overnight by the enthusiastic review by Théophile Gautier of the *Cock Fight*, shown at the Salon of 1847. This type of ancient genre scene executed with literal realism became known as the "Neo-Greek" or *pompéiste* style and Gérôme was recognized as its principal exponent.

Two-thirds of Gérôme's oeuvre deals with subjects of Near Eastern or North African inspiration and his numerous visits to those lands provided opportunities for direct observation of the people and their customs. The *Snake Charmer* is a genre scene depicting an Egyptian coffee house; it is rendered with a detached objectivity that is characteristic of Gérôme's orientalism. The snake charmer or *hawee*, his youthful assistant and the two snakes perform for the interested audience. The vessels, baskets, tattered carpet and instruments are all authentic. The sense of immediacy of the scene is enhanced by the shadowy light of the interior and the flashes of bright sunlight on the high wall. The old man standing playing the *oud*, for whom there is a preliminary drawing (Claremont, California, G. Ackerman coll.), reinforces the painting's verticalty, the preferred format for Gérôme's Near Eastern pictures.

E.P.C.

The Snake Charmer, circa 1880-1890
oil on canvas
91.5 x 73.6 cm./36 x 29 inches
Gift of Mr. and Mrs.
Chapman H. Hyams,
15.13

21   Jehan Georges Vibert (1840-1902)

Vibert was one of the most popular French artists of the later nineteenth century in both France and in America. He was greatly admired for his mocking wit, equally evident in his short plays, and his detailed realism, the precision of which was facilitated by his frequent use of panel for a picture's support. Vibert's academic training began at age sixteen and his first Salon exhibition was in 1863. His early paintings were of historical and religious themes, but he soon turned to a gentle satirical tone, often focusing on ecclesiastics in comical genre situations.

The *Cardinals' Friendly Chat* depicts two ecclesiastics who enjoy an animated conversation over wine and elegant cakes. Vibert makes an intentional ironic reference to the eucharist with the biscuit being soaked in the wine. This comic mode creates a theatrical feeling that is clearly related to Vibert's stage productions. The playful mockery of the princes of the Church is taken further by the setting of their intimate afternoon party - it is the Turkish Boudoir of Marie-Antoinette in the castle of Fontainebleau. The furnishings in the Empire style were added by the Empress Josephine in 1805.

E.P.C.

The Cardinals' Friendly Chat, circa 1880

oil on panel

73.7 x 97.8 cm./29 x 38 ½ inches

Gift of Mr. and Mrs. Chapman H. Hyams,

15.27

22 William Adolphe Bouguereau (1825-1905)

Bouguereau's name, like that of Gérôme, has become synonymous with French academic painting of the second half of the nineteenth century. Immensely popular with the throngs at the annual Salons, Bouguereau, after 1870, became a favorite painter of American collectors, over even the much-admired Barbizon landscapists. He was one of the most powerful figures in official French art circles, but after his death his name fell into relative obscurity, his work considered too sentimental for the emerging modern age. Only in the past twenty years has interest been revived in Bouguereau as the supreme academician in the great age of the Salon.

Had Bouguereau followed his parents' wishes, he would have remained in the world of commerce. Through the kind offices of an uncle and his own efforts as a portrait painter, Bouguereau was able to study at the Ecole des Beaux-Arts in Bordeaux. He arrived in Paris in 1846 and entered the Beaux-Arts as a student of Picot.

In 1850 he won the *prix de Rome*; by 1859 he was made a member of the Legion of Honor.

Most of Bouguereau's Salon pictures are nudes, religious subjects and figures from classical history or mythology. *Whisperings of Love* is more of a genre piece, executed in the highly finished, realistic style of the "Neo-Greeks." Historical authenticity is attempted with the Greek chiton and the protogeometric amphora. The reduced color range and the idealized beauty of the young woman are noted characteristics of Bouguereau's later style. The sentimentality of the artist, so highly regarded by some and harshly criticized by others, is expressed here through the large, searching eyes of the maiden. She appears vulnerable, yet somehow receptive, to the amorous stirrings aroused by the whispers of the playful Cupid.

E.P.C.

Whisperings of Love, 1889
oil on canvas
157.5 x 92.7 cm./62 x 36 ½ inches
Gift of Mr. and Mrs. Chapman H. Hyams,
15.6

23   Edgar Degas (1834-1917)

Perhaps the most well-known French painting of the New Orleans collection, Degas' portrait of his sister-in-law (and first cousin) was painted in New Orleans in December, 1872, during the artist's five-month stay in his mother's native city. Like other Impressionist painters, Degas found the years 1870-1872 to be trying ones. They had become dispirited by or some even physically wounded in the Franco-Prussian War, relationships with dealers were sometimes turning difficult and the Salon of 1872, for which Degas, Monet, Pissarro and Sisley submitted nothing, appeared to these painters as more political than artistic in nature. Many of the Impressionists left Paris temporarily in 1872: Degas came to New Orleans, where his uncle, Michel Musson, was prominent in the cotton business, and his brothers Achille and René were wine importers.

In New Orleans Degas painted about fifteen portraits of family members, all portrayed in interiors (he found the light too intense for his eyes that had been weakened in the war). Degas felt a particular sympathy for the blind Estelle (1843-1909), wife of his brother René, portrayed here immediately before the birth of her fourth child. His description of her in a letter relates her brave acceptance of the handicap, though it ends, "she is almost without hope." Two other portraits of Estelle were produced during this short visit (Washington, National Gallery of Art and Paris, Musée d'Orsay); the New Orleans picture is the largest and most monumental in conception.

Estelle is depicted arranging flowers in a shaded room. The sketchy ground of reds and browns creates an aura of darkness emanating from her form, probably a reference to her blindness. Degas also emphasizes the sense of touch with the woman's hands tentatively touching the flowers. Her face is silvery grey and is illuminated not from the window, but from a source of light to the left, creating a sense of ineffable mystery. The surface is then enlivened with the greens, whites, reds and yellows of the bouquet. The portrait's unfinished state reveals how Degas' painting process was more closely approaching the Impressionist aesthetic in the early 1870s.

E.P.C.

Portrait of Estelle Musson, 1872
oil on canvas
100 x 137 cm./39 ½ x 54 inches
Museum Purchase through Public Subscription,
65.1

24   Edgar Degas (1834-1917)

During the first decade of his artistic career Degas painted portraits and historical themes. Eventually however, to find subject matter for his paintings, the artist turned to contemporary life. He studied people in action going about their work; jockeys, milliners, laundresses, opera singers and dancers. Gradually as Degas' interest in the opera and theater grew, dancers assumed a background position similar to that allotted to landscape in his earlier painting. Then, with the picture *Musiciens de l'Orchestre*, the dancer suddenly occupied center stage. This subject became a major concern of the artist in the years between 1875 and 1890 during which time he began experimenting with pastels as a primary medium. Degas spent many hours attending ballet classes in order to observe the struggling young "rats" of the Paris Opera and to sketch them in class and on the stage.

Dancer in Green shows a young girl waiting in the wings during a performance. In depicting the dancer, the artist employs several of his favorite devices including averting the face in half-profile; positioning the figure high up in the picture plane; using back-lighting and selectively viewing empty space as an important part of the composition. He also executed an oblique view with exaggerated recession, a device he adopted after studying Japanese prints.

J.G.C.

Dancer in Green, circa 1878
pastel on paper
48.3 x 29.2 cm. / 18 ¼ x 11 ½ inches
Gift of Charles C. Henderson
in memory of Nancy S. Henderson,
74.282

25   Eugène-Louis Boudin (1824-1898)

Boudin's landscape art spanned over half a century and its influence on the plein-air painting of the Impressionists was profound. Most of his paintings depict marine subjects; it was with the sea and vast skies along the coast that Boudin could experiment with what he himself called his "thirst for light." In the 1840s while working in a framer's shop in Le Havre, he met J.F. Millet, Thomas Couture and Constant Troyon who encouraged him to take up painting. By 1857 he had his first exhibition in Paris and a year later he met Claude Monet, who often spoke of the debt he owed Boudin in learning to capture the clarity and force of natural light. In the 1860s Boudin began painting the "beau monde" at the fashionable seaside resort of Trouville; ten years later, his work began to sell more easily. He was a constant contributor to the annual Salons, but also exhibited with the Impressionists in 1874.

The famous art dealer Paul Durand-Ruel became the champion of Boudin's painting in the 1880s, which assisted greatly in securing the artist's reputation and financial well-being.

Toward 1889 with the pressure of success and the death of his wife, Boudin endured a brief period of artistic weakness demonstrable in his rather melancholy views of Caudebec. As a cure, he began to travel, since changes of scenery had always spurred his artistic talents in the past. Searching for new subjects to paint as well as a different visual goal, he traveled home to Normandy in 1891. *Landscape in Normandy* is a record of this artistic renewal which lasted throughout Boudin's later travels to Venice and Honfleur, and in fact, until his death in 1898.

E.P.C./J.G.C.

Landscape in Normandy, 1891

oil on canvas

48.2 x 58.4 cm. / 19 x 23 inches

Gift of the Armand Hammer Foundation,

70.14

26   Alfred Sisley (1839-1899)

Sisley's origins were Parisian and comfortably middle-class. Bored with his business training, he was able to persuade his parents to allow him to enter the studio of the academic painter Charles Gleyre in 1862. There he met Claude Monet, Pierre Renoir and Frédéric Bazille: the four young artists opposed to the traditional methods of painting soon formed their own group. They would become the central core of revolutionary painters who would be known as the Impressionists after their first exhibition independent of the Salon in 1874. Their goal was to recreate the natural phenomenon of vision through colors of paint and their relationship to each other on the surface of the canvas. Sisley was the most consistent of the entire group, exhibiting at all of the Impressionist shows and maintaining his delicate and poetic view of nature. Sisley's work was subject to fewer disparaging remarks by the public than that of his colleagues, but his last years were spent in dire poverty.

Sisley, like Monet, was interested in the changing colors of nature and effects of atmosphere, particularly at moments of seasonal change. Thus the focus of this landscape is on the springtime blossoming of the trees and the freshness of the earth, conveyed by the use of greens, pinks and violets. Along with Camille Pissarro, Sisley was concerned with establishing deep, perspectival space, usually given an understandable scale with the addition of one or two figures. His style is airy and light because his brushstrokes and forms within the image are less dense than are those of other Impressionist painters. Sisley has chosen a wet, overcast day, when colors appear more saturated, to paint this small valley (now called Véneux-les-Sablons) near the town of Moret on the edge of the Fontainebleau forest.

E.P.C.

Springtime in Véneux-Nadon, 1882
oil on canvas
44.5 x 61 cm./ 17 ½ x 24 inches
Mrs. Frederick M. Stafford Collection

27   Claude Monet (1840-1926)

The primacy of Claude Monet among the painters of the Impressionist movement and his position as a cornerstone in the development of modern art are well-established facts. His first encounter with the art of painting came through his contact with Boudin at Le Havre in 1858. In the 1860s came his period of discontent with academic painting in Charles Gleyre's studio, his first Salon exhibitions and closer relationships with other young painters seeking new directions. Monet exhibited with this cohesive group of radical painters throughout the 1870s, his style constantly evolving during this period. Critical appraisal of the new art movement was, at times, virulent; it was not until 1889 that success came to Monet after many hardships and much frustration.

Water is a recurrent motif in Monet's compositions and appears here in *House on the Old Bridge at Vernon*. In previous landscape painting, water was depicted in a fixed and regularized manner as a mirror-like reflective area. In Monet's pictures however, water no longer has a fixed, unvarying character, but rather, assumes a variety of appearances. This appearance is dependent upon Monet's other major concern, depicting the atmospheric conditions of the landscape at the time during which he was painting it.

In this work, these concerns are used to convey the impression of a stormy day. The palette is dark, the colors being muted and almost muddy. The overcast sky is dominated by dense, grey cloud masses. The body of water appears to be quite agitated with white-crested waves stirred up by an impending storm. Although a broken brushstroke is characteristic of Monet's work and is used throughout the image, the strokes composing the area of water appear to have been dragged or slashed through very thick pigment. Rather than acting as a reflective surface, this water is dark and opaque. Monet's working method was one based upon observation rather than invention. In respecting his perceptions and refusing to embellish or idealize, Monet has captured that moment before the onslaught, when the storm is yet a threat.

S.E.S.

House on the Old Bridge of Vernon, circa 1884

oil on canvas

59.4 x 80 cm./ 23 ¾ x 32 inches

Private Collection

28   Claude Monet (1840-1926)

By 1870 Monet had restricted himself almost completely to landscapes painted *en plein air*. He had abandoned his early experiments with the painting of tonal values and concentrated on the representation of light and hue, rendering harmonies of color hue in varying conditions of light. For much of his life, Monet was restless and moved through France, the Low Countries and England to paint various landscapes. In 1883 he settled at Giverny where he remained for most of the rest of his life.

This view of the farmhouses on the hillside of Giverny is very nearly a study in opposites from his earlier *House on the Old Bridge at Vernon*. It depicts a brightly lit scene of the type more usually associated with Impressionist landscapes. *Rooftops, Giverny* is a compendium of the various means by which Monet translated his visual impressions into paint. He was intent upon arresting the fleeting moment, upon capturing its ephemeral effects of light and color. This view of Giverny is almost dissolved in the flickering network of color patches that is the usual result of his rapid and intuitive working method. The bright multi-colored foreground is composed of quick, short brushstrokes applied at various angles to each other. The middleground, dominated by blues and greens, is painted with broader, more regular strokes. The distant hills are painted in a smooth, slightly wavy manner, while the sky is almost unmodulated. Monet thus approximates the varying intensity of sunlight and the effects of aerial perspective in his attempt to close the gap between perception and the painted image.

E.P.C./S.E.S.

Rooftops, Giverny, 1886
oil on canvas
65 x 81 cm./ 25 ½ x 32 ¼ inches
Mrs. Frederick M. Stafford Collection

29   Camille Pissarro (1830-1903)

Pissarro's role in the Impressionist movement was that of generator and constant supporter. From the time he entered the Académie Suisse in 1856, where he first met Monet, Pissarro knew and worked with all the future Impressionists, as well as with Cézanne, Gauguin, Van Gogh and eventually Signac and Seurat. As a young painter, he took part in the famous Salon des Refusés of 1863 and later was the only artist to show at all eight of the Impressionist exhibitions. Pissarro's early paintings bear a close stylistic affinity to those of Monet, but while the latter came to dissolve material substance into color and light, Pissarro always sought to depict solid forms in a traditionally constructed space. Pissarro's most experimental period came in the 1880s when he joined Signac and Seurat in their scientific approach to painting, called divisionism or pointillism, through which a deliberate and systematic application of small dots of pure color would create an image in the eye of the viewer. During the last decade of Pissarro's life, when he finally received public recognition, he returned to an impressionist style, but with a lighter palette and greater purity of color.

Pissarro spent much of his later life painting at Eragny. This painting typifies the Impressionists' manner of filling shadows with color, in this case the trees' shadows on the snow are filled with violets and mauves. The influence of the pointillist style is visible in the middle ground in the application of small touches of violets, reds and orange; the sky, however, displays the hooked brushstroke found more often in impressionist works. Pissarro carefully constructs an easily receding space with fences, aligned trees and a winding footpath. The seasonal light is then captured by the pale yellow winter sun on the horizon.

E.P.C.

Sun Setting at Eragny, 1894

oil on canvas

61 x 82.6 cm./24 x 32 ½ inches

Mrs. Frederick M. Stafford Collection

30 Camille Pissarro (1830-1903)

In the last years of his life, Pissarro divided his time between Eragny, where he painted landscapes during the warmer seasons, and Paris. In the capital he rented an apartment on the rue de Rivoli from which he could have an elevated view of the streets and parks below. Around 1900 he began his famous series of the Tuileries, the Louvre and the Pont Neuf, to which this painting belongs. This work does not investigate the bustle of the crowded streets, but focuses rather on the effects of the wintery atmosphere and the bird's-eye perspective of the depopulated park. As in most of his paintings, Pissarro has structured his space with easily readable segments, resulting in a gentle recession of space to a horizon more distant than is typical of the work of other Impressionists.

E.P.C.

Garden of the Tuileries in Winter, 1900
oil on canvas
66 x 91.4 cm./ 26 x 36 inches
Mrs. Frederick M. Stafford Collection

31   Gustave Caillebotte (1848-1894)

Caillebotte was raised in an affluent Parisian family, studied law and served in the military before entering the *Ecole des Beaux-Arts* in 1873 through the influence of the academic painter Léon Bonnat. In 1874 he associated himself with the Impressionists who were then under intense criticism from academic circles. He exhibited with that group several times and was an avid collector of their more daring works. His own paintings of urban subject matter were consistent with the Impressionist style. His plunging perspectives of Parisian streets are his most innovative works. After the Impressionists split up in 1882, Caillebotte spent most of his time at his country home in Petit-Gennevillers, near his friend Monet at Argenteuil. Caillebotte's collection of Impressionist works was eventually given to the state and is now housed in the Musée d'Orsay in Paris.

Caillebotte was an amateur horticulturist and floral still-lifes became more important in his oeuvre after his departure from Paris. At this time his technique loosened, though here his flowers appear densely arranged over a large portion of the picture field. The painting pulsates with life and color harmonies and demonstrates the artist's firm mastery of the Impressionist style. This still-life is dated about 1887 when most of Caillebotte's painting focused on his house and garden at Petit-Gennevilliers.

E.P.C.

Bouquet of China Asters and Sunflowers,
circa 1887
oil on canvas
62.8 x 50.2 cm./ 23 ¾ x 19 ¾ inches
Gift of Dr. and Mrs. Richard W. Levy,
77.48

32   Pierre Auguste Renoir (1841-1919)

Renoir began his long artistic career as an apprentice to a porcelain painter in Paris. In 1862 he was enrolled at the Beaux-Arts as a student of Charles Gleyre in whose studio he met the other central figures of the Impressionist movement. He was soon attracted to the colorism of Delacroix, the modernism of Courbet and the painterly qualities of Edouard Manet. In the late 1860s Renoir was most interested in painting light, and his work is almost indistinguishable from that of Monet, with whom he worked quite closely. But he is more often remembered for the sensuality and vibrancy of his colors, especially his blues and reds. Renoir was the most instrumental of the Impressionists in creating the new image of the urban, middle-class society happily enjoying their leisure time.

Renoir began to break from the Impressionist group around 1881, when he came in contact with classical art. He felt that their predominant interest in color and light over line and composition threatened a loss of the basic human qualities inherent in the classical tradition of art. His own painting came to rely more on line and descriptive detail, with a corresponding emphasis on the human form. Renoir's oeuvre, more than that of any of the Impressionists, includes a great deal of monumental figures, especially women.

Seamstress at Window is a late work and falls into the category of a genre painting. The model is undoubtedly Gabrielle, the young woman who became Renoir's housekeeper in 1895. The reds and oranges of his palette, with the sense of light emanating from the exterior, provide warmth and glow to the image. Renoir's purpose here seems to be the creation of a sense of domestic tranquility, most likely reflecting the old artist's home life.

E.P.C.

Seamstress at Window, circa 1910
oil on canvas
64.8 x 54.6 cm./ 25 ½ x 21 ½ inches
Gift of Mr. Charles C. Henderson
in memory of Margaret Henderson,
80.179

33 Paul Gauguin (1848-1903)

Gauguin is often considered the most romantically heroic of the Impressionist and Post-Impressionist painters because he rejected family, career and country in pursuit of the purification of his art. After traveling extensively in his youth, he took up a career in the Paris stock exchange and painted as an amateur, having a Corot-inspired landscape accepted in the Salon of 1876. Three years later he met Pissarro who guided him toward the Impressionist movement; in 1879 Gauguin was asked to exhibit with this group. By 1883 Gauguin had become totally involved in painting and two years later he left his family to concentrate solely upon his art. He travelled to Brittany, Provence and Martinique where the brilliance of the natural colors greatly affected his work. By 1890, before his voyage to Tahiti, Gauguin had abandoned the Impressionist style for the new, more abstract aesthetic, called Synthetism, which he had developed in association with Emile Bernard. They rejected naturalism, preferring instead to express ideas, moods, and emotions through a stylized aesthetic language reminiscent of medieval glass and enamel work with its strong, simple colors separated by black lines.

Gauguin painted *Haymaking II* late in 1888, soon after a visit with Van Gogh in Arles and during his second stay in the Breton village of Pont-Aven. This painting is actually an earlier and smaller version of the painting *Haymaking in Brittany* (Paris, Musée d'Orsay) which depicts the same field (which belonged to the Derout-Lollichon family). This is one of the last of Gauguin's paintings that can be associated with the Impressionist style, though the brushstroke is already becoming longer and more regular, and the color choice more subjective. The life of the painting comes from the resonance of juxtaposed colors rather than from the intensity of individual hues. The subject and viewpoint, however, are still consistent with the Impressionism of the 1880s.

E.P.C./S.E.S.

Haymaking II, 1888
oil on canvas
50.2 x 64 cm./ 19 ¾ x 24 inches
Mrs. Frederick M. Stafford Collection

34 Paul Gauguin (1848-1903)

Gauguin's rejection of western civilization is prefigured in his powerful portrayal of Eve. Whereas the *fin de siècle* was permeated by a general yearning for a more natural life, one uncorrupted by modernity, Gauguin's was more extreme, leading him to idealize the primitive and to look upon western civilization as a disease. His desire to escape everything that was artificial and conventional led him to attempt to assimilate various "primitive" cultures and although he found his ultimate escape in Tahiti, he found his initial experience with a simpler culture in the Breton region of France. Gauguin was profoundly impressed by the devotion of the Bretons and the more primitive ideas, rites, and myths of their popular religious culture. The figure of Eve, symbolic of the original clash between natural freedom and societal convention, is an appropriate subject of Gauguin's attraction to religious myth and pursuit of elemental human feelings he thought repressed by conventions of middle class society.

Gauguin has portrayed the primal terror and shame of Eve using his newly developed Synthetist pictorial idiom. Eve is composed of flattened planes bounded by contour lines. She clasps her hands over her face and ears as if shutting out the external world. Although related to a similar *Eve* (San Antonio, Marion Koogler McNay Art Institute), who cringes below the Tree of Knowledge around which slithers the fateful serpent, this *Eve* is removed from any narrative framework. The rectangular frame barely contains her painful figure, making the sense of isolation almost claustraphobic. This lack of the specific biblical context makes her an even more powerful symbol of fundamental fear.

Gauguin's concern for a simplicity of emotion and human feeling and interest in a simpler style and culture is made complete by the source for his *Eve*. He used a Peruvian mummy, exhibited in the 1880s in Paris' ethnological museum, which is bound in a crouching position with its skeletal arms and hands raised to its skull, mirroring the pose of *Eve*. This strange relic of primitive terror is even more appropriate for Gauguin's use because of its association with his personal heritage since his mother's family was part Peruvian.

S.E.S.

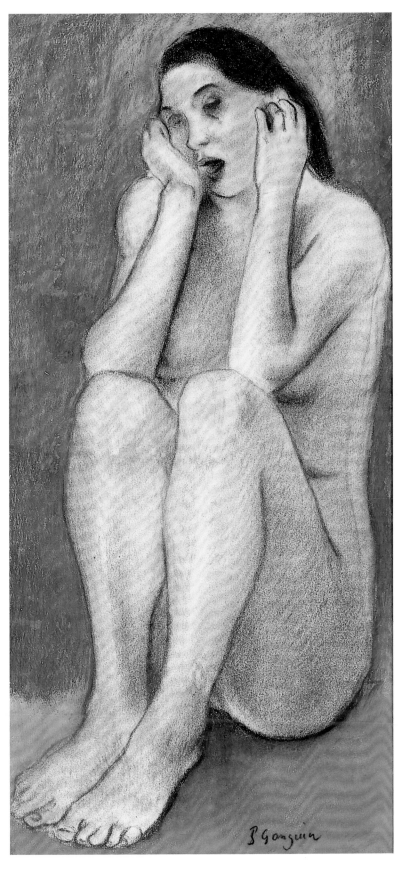

Eve Bretonne, circa 1889
pastel on paper
52.5 x 27.5 cm./21 x 11 inches
Private Collection

35 Pierre Bonnard (1867-1947)

A generation younger than the Impressionists, Bonnard was a painter and lithographer. While studying law in Paris, he began painting at the Académie Julian, where he met the other young artists who would found the Nabis group. They took their name from the Hebrew word for prophet and held a common admiration for Gauguin and the highly decorative quality of line and color in his more abstract works. Bonnard spent much of his earlier career designing posters and book illustrations, using bold, two-dimensional designs in black against a neutral ground. He later developed a painting style resplendent with bright hues and a magical, colored light.

In 1891 Bonnard created the design for a commercial poster advertising *France Champagne*. It was an immediate success and helped popularize what has come to be known as the art nouveau style. When Alfred and Thadée Natanson took over the publication of avant-garde literary and art magazine called *La Revue Blanche*, they called upon Bonnard for illustrations and, in 1894, the design for a poster. This gouache is the study for the lithographic poster. A street urchin, bent over, distorts his face as he loudly hawks his journal. He points behind himself where a woman stands, her large eyes coquettishly peering out from her stylish belle époque costume. The model is believed to have been Marthe Méligny (née Maria Boursin), Bonnard's mistress and later his wife. A third figure, seen from behind, is a man wearing a top hat and bending over to read or buy an issue of the magazine at a newsstand. Few changes appear in the resulting poster, though the image is flattened and the newsman's cravat becomes patterned.

E.P.C.

Study for La Revue Blanche *Poster*, 1894
gouache on paper
79.4 x 59.7 cm. / 31 ¼ x 23 ½ inches
Gift of Mr. and Mrs. Frederick M. Stafford,
76.421

36 Edouard Vuillard (1868-1940)

Although Vuillard is perhaps best known for his role as a founding member of the Nabis, an influential offshoot of the Symbolist movement, this scene is illustrative of the body of work that earned him further description as an intimist. His work garnered this title due to its consistently small-scale nature and concentration upon evocative depictions of his family and friends in familiar surroundings, these almost always interiors. It is in these intimate interiors of the decade between 1890 and 1900 that Vuillard's artistic sensibility and pictorial construction manifest themselves at their most sophisticated and complex.

Vuillard constructed these interiors to evoke his life in a visual shorthand. They not only depict familiar rooms, but they also convey his feelings towards the characters who inhabit them. The interior functioned for Vuillard as a potential metaphor for himself, an inner space at once self-controlled and removed from the world as well as fecund with possibility. The interior operated as the subject through which he could best explore the complex emotional and intellectual issues central to a beginning painter's development.

The space in this, as in most of Vuillard's interior scenes, is crowded, almost claustraphobic, and difficult to decipher. The image illustrates one of the ideas that remained central to the psychological scrutiny of his art, the relationship between form and color and their power to convey meaning. The psychological impact of this image upon the viewer is certainly jarring. The viewer's access to the space is both directed and denied by the form of the bureau jutting in from the right. The space, being dominated by a single tonal character, appears ambiguous. However, it retains Vuillard's usual structure of contrast in the formation of the background wall through a series of rectangles varied in pattern and color. Such elusiveness of structure, form, and thereby meaning, ultimately creates an enigma of Vuillard's intimate interiors, thus making them so compelling.

S.E.S.

Interior Scene, circa 1900
pastel on paper
58.7 x 46.4 cm. / 23 ½ x 18 ¼ inches
Muriel Bultman Francis Collection,
86.312

37   Odilon Redon (1840-1916)

Although he was their exact contemporary, Redon's strong imaginative bent put him out of sympathy with the Impressionists' artistic aims. His belief that an art of wider reference than Impressionism was needed led him during the 1870s to evolve a pictorial language in which may be seen the essence of Symbolism. Symbolism was a loosely organized movement of artists both visual — Puvis de Chavannes, Gustave Moreau — and literary — Stéphane Mallarmé, J.-K. Huysmans — who shared a similar attitude of protest. Theirs was a revolt against the scientific rationalism and materialism that had developed through the nineteenth century. From the Symbolist belief that a picture is neither simply an arrangement of lines and colors nor a direct transcript from nature, but the manifestation of another order of meaning, spring Redon's visionary images.

Beasts at the Bottom of the Sea allowed Redon to combine his love of brilliant, jewel-like color with his continuing fascination with the animal world. Using variegated textures and directional movements of shimmering pastels ranging from blues to greens to yellows, Redon has evoked a mysterious, aqueous world. Suspended in it are fanciful imaginary creatures who playfully twist and turn in arabesques that enliven the composition. Using such playful forms and alluring colors, Redon has transformed the underwater depths from a cold, alien environment into an enticing and attractive image, strengthening its appeal by transposing a smiling anthropomorphic face onto the zoomorphic creature.

S.E.S.

Beasts at the Bottom of the Sea,
circa 1900-1905
pastel on paper
60 x 49.5 cm. / 24 x 19 ¾ inches
Muriel Bultman Francis Collection,
83.69

38 Odilon Redon (1840-1916)

"I think I have created an expressive, suggestive, indeterminate art. Suggestive art is the irradiation of divine plastic elements, brought together, combined with a view to causing dreams that are enlightened and exalted by it, while giving rise to thought."

In their imprecise and yet evocative nature, Redon's words themselves reveal the mechanism of his art. His images never depict a specific visual perception or objective observation. Rather, they function as imaginary or visionary counterparts to his experiences. Redon combines separate elements in ambiguous yet carefully balanced, visually expressive designs in order to create works of mystification and suggestion, not of allegory or ideas.

During the first part of his career, Redon worked almost exclusively in the black and white media of charcoal and lithography, but in about 1890 he began to explore the possibilities of color.

In his subsequent pictures he uses pastels and oils to transform his subject matter into suggestive arrangements of forms and textures that produce a state of thoughtfulness in the viewer. *The Butterflies' Dream* illustrates his interest in the intrinsic expressiveness of color, an interest which ultimately led to his acknowledgement as one of the foremost colorists of France. The butterflies that float against Redon's shimmering color fields reveal his fascination with the animal world as well as his continued link with everyday things. Under the influence of his artistic vision however, these mundane things are invested with some allusive or metaphorical quality. Indeed, it was this ability to create through metaphor a magic out of humdrum reality that caused Redon to be called "the Mallarmé of painting."

S.E.S.

The Butterflies' Dream, circa 1910-15
oil on panel
39.4 x 73.7 cm. / 15 ½ x 29 inches
Gift of Muriel Bultman Francis,
86.284

Index of Artist and Titles